CHILDREN'S
BIBLE
CLASSICS

DAVID AND GOLIATH

Tommy
NELSON™

Thomas Nelson, Inc.
Nashville

Published in Nashville, Tennessee, by Tommy Nelson™,
a division of Thomas Nelson, Inc.

Originally published in 1993 by
Thomas Nelson Publishers, Nashville, Tennessee.

**Story retold by Bill Yenne
and Timothy Jacobs**

Edited by Lynne Piade. Art and design direction by Bill
Yenne. Illustrated by Pete Avdoulos, Mark Busacca, Emi
Fukawa, Victor Lee, Wendy K. Lee, Douglas Scott, Peggy
Smith, Alexandr Stolin, Vadim Vahrameev, Hanako
Wakiyama, Nelson Wang, and Bill Yenne.

Produced by
Bluewood Books (A Division of The Siyeh Group, Inc.)
P.O. Box 689, San Mateo, CA 94401

David and Goliath.
   p.   cm.—(Children's Bible Classics)
  ISBN 0-8407-4913-9 (TR)
  ISBN 0-8407-4911-2 (MM)
  1. David, King of Israel—Juvenile literature. 2. Goliath
(Biblical giant)—Juvenile literature. 3. Bible Stories,
English—O.T. Samuel, 1st. I. Thomas Nelson
 Publishers. II. Series.
BS580.D3D38 1993
222'.4309505—dc20   93-24836
                                   CIP
                                   AC

Printed and bound in the United States of America

97 98 99 00 01 02 03 LBM 9 8 7 6 5 4 3

DAVID AND GOLIATH

Long ago, there lived a good man named Samuel. He was a prophet and a man of peace and the people loved him. God told Samuel to choose a man named Saul to be King of Israel.

Saul became king and at first he was a good man, but sometimes he didn't do what God told him. This made Samuel angry.

Samuel was sad. He loved King Saul, but he was sad because Saul had disobeyed God's commands. God told Samuel to find someone new to be king.

God told Samuel to go see a man named Jesse. God would choose one of Jesse's sons to be the new king. Jesse had eight sons and he brought seven of them to meet Samuel.

But, one by one, God turned down each one of the seven.

Finally Samuel asked Jesse, "Don't you have another son?" Jesse answered, "Yes, I do—my youngest son David is with our sheep out in the hills."
Samuel told Jesse to get the boy.

God told Samuel that this boy would one day be king of Israel. Samuel gave David a special blessing and then returned home.

David went back to watch over the sheep. They still needed David to protect them with his sling when the lions or bears came around.

David was also a very good musician. When things were peaceful, he liked to play his lyre, which is something like a harp. He played beautiful tunes, making up words to go with them. Many of his words are recorded in the Book of Psalms.

The most famous of David's psalms is Psalm 23, which is also known as the Shepherd's Psalm:

"The Lord is my Shepherd; I shall not want.
He makes me to lie down in green pastures:
He leads me beside the still waters.
He restores my soul;
He leads me in the paths of righteousness
    for His name's sake.
Yea, though I walk through the valley of the shadow
    of death
I will fear no evil; for You art with me;
Your rod and Your staff, they comfort me.
You prepare a table before me in the
    presence of mine enemies;
You anoint my head with oil; my cup runs over.
Surely goodness and mercy shall follow me
    All the days of my life:
And I will dwell in the house of the Lord
    Forever."

Meanwhile, King Saul was unhappy.
The Spirit of God had left him and he
could not rest.

Saul decided that he wanted someone to come and play music to cheer him up. He asked for David. David's music comforted him and he felt much happier. Whenever Saul was sad David would play for him.

But then there came a war with the Philistines. Saul had to call for an army. David's brothers joined Saul's army but David was still too young. He went back to care for his father's sheep.

The Israelites were afraid because the Philistine army had one very big and very strong soldier. His name was Goliath. He was so tall he looked like a giant.

No man in the army, not even King Saul, dared to go out and fight Goliath. Saul tried to get some of his better soldiers to try, but they were all too scared. Even David's brothers were afraid.

One day, David came to visit his brothers. He was not afraid of Goliath. He was angry at Goliath for insulting God and for scaring everybody.

"If no one else will go, then I will go out and fight this enemy," said David.

The soldiers brought David before King Saul and the King said to David, "You cannot fight this giant. You are too young."

David answered, "I am only a shepherd, but I have fought with lions and bears when they tried to steal my sheep. I am not afraid to fight. The Lord will save me from this enemy, for I will fight for the Lord and His people."

Saul admired David's courage. He told one of his soldiers to put the king's own armor on David. But Saul's armor was much too big for David.

David decided to use his sling, and picked up five smooth stones from a nearby brook. When Goliath saw David, he just laughed. Goliath couldn't believe this boy was going to fight him. But David said, "God will help me."

David chose one smooth stone from his pouch. He took careful aim and slung the stone at Goliath.

The stone struck Goliath square on the forehead with a loud *thwack*. The giant fell with a *crash*.
David had trusted in the Lord and he won.

When Goliath's army saw him fall, they ran away in fear. King Saul was very proud of David. David was a hero to the King's soldiers and they celebrated his victory over Goliath.